W9-BRB-241

WHITE HOUSE INSIDERS

What's It Like to Live in the
WHITE HOUSE?

BY KATHLEEN CONNORS

Gareth Stevens
PUBLISHING

Please visit our website, www.garethstevens.com. For a free color catalog of all our high-quality books, call toll free 1-800-542-2595 or fax 1-877-542-2596.

Library of Congress Cataloging-in-Publication Data

Connors, Kathleen.
What's it like to live in the White House? / by Kathleen Connors.
p. cm. — (White House insiders)
Includes index.
ISBN 978-1-4824-1111-9 (pbk.)
ISBN 978-1-4824-1112-6 (6-pack)
ISBN 978-1-4824-1110-2 (library binding)
1. White House (Washington, D.C.) — Juvenile literature. 2. Washington (D.C.) — Buildings, structures, etc.
Juvenile literature. 3. Presidents — United States — Juvenile literature.
I. Connors, Kathleen. II. Title.
F204.W5 C66 2015
975.3—d23

First Edition

Published in 2015 by
Gareth Stevens Publishing
111 East 14th Street, Suite 349
New York, NY 10003

Copyright © 2015 Gareth Stevens Publishing

Designer: Nick Domiano
Editor: Kristen Rajczak

Photo credits: Cover, p. 1 (Oval Office) spirit of america/Shutterstock.com; cover, p. 1 (White House) iStock/Thinkstock.com; cover, p. 1 (Lincoln Bedroom) The White House/Hulton Archive/Getty Images; p. 5 Happyme22/Wikimedia Commons; p. 7 Mondadori/Mondadori Portfolio/Getty Images; p. 9 Nicholas Kamm/AFP/Getty Images; p. 11 Bill O'Leary/The Washington Post/Getty Images; p. 13 Mandel Ngan/AFP/Getty Images; p. 15 Artur Widak/AFP/Getty Images; p. 17 Raymond Boyd/Michael Ochs Archives/Getty Images; p. 19 Paul J. Richards/AFP/Getty Images; p. 20 Jewel Samad/AFP/Getty Images.

Printed in the United States of America

CPSIA compliance information: Batch #CS15GS: For further information contact Gareth Stevens, New York, New York at 1-800-542-2595.

Contents

Words in the glossary appear in **bold** type the first time they are used in the text.

White Home

The White House has had many names, including the Executive Mansion. It was President Theodore Roosevelt who officially named it the White House in 1901, though it had been known by that name for many years. The White House is found at 1600 Pennsylvania Avenue in the capital of the United States, Washington, DC.

So much happens at the White House, from US lawmaking to agreements between the United States and other countries. It's also home to the president and First Lady!

The Inside Scoop

George Washington chose where in Washington, DC, the White House would be built, but he never lived there.

Construction of the White House finished in 1800.
John Adams was the first president to live in the

All Business

A big part of life in the White House happens in the West Wing. That's where the president's staff works. President Theodore Roosevelt began construction on the office building that would become today's West Wing in 1902. It was connected to the White House **Residence** by a walkway.

After Roosevelt, President William Taft added to the building, including the Oval Office. President Franklin Roosevelt gave the West Wing a second floor and moved the Oval Office so he could have more privacy.

The Inside Scoop

Theodore Roosevelt needed to build the West Wing because his office was near his bedroom—and his six children could always find him there!

This photograph of President John F. Kennedy shows that even when at work in the Oval Office, the president's children might still be around!

The Residence

The president's family is called the First Family. They live on the second and third floors of the East Wing of the White House. The East Wing was first built in 1902 and became its present size with additions made in 1942.

The president's bedroom is in the East Wing. Any children would have bedrooms there, too. First Lady Jacqueline Kennedy added a family kitchen and dining room for the First Family in 1961. The First Lady's office is often found in the East Wing, as well.

The Inside Scoop

Before the middle of the 20th century, it was common for extended family to live with the First Family. President Ulysses S. Grant's father-in-law lived at the White House, as did President Harry Truman's mother-in-law.

First Lady Michelle Obama's mother Marian Robinson wasn't planning to live at the White House at first, but there's plenty of room, so she did. Marian helped out with the Obamas' daughters, Malia and Sasha.

Lots of Room

One of the most famous rooms of the White House is in the East Wing—the Lincoln Bedroom. Though President Abraham Lincoln used it as an office and never slept there, lots of other people have. The Lincoln Bedroom is commonly used as a guest room in the White House Residence. British Prime Minister Winston Churchill stayed there!

The third floor of the White House's East Wing is often where the First Family spends time together. There's a place to exercise, a music room, and a game room.

The Inside Scoop

Some of the coolest parts of the White House include the bowling alley, outdoor pool, tennis and basketball courts, and movie theater.

The Lincoln Bedroom also has a sitting room and bathroom attached.

Pricey Place to Live

In 2013, the cost to run the White House was said to be about $1.4 billion. The First Family lives there for free. However, they have to pay for their own daily items, such as toothpaste. Nancy Reagan said she was surprised the first time she was presented with a bill for her food while at home in the White House!

And the fancy parties the president throws? The First Family pays for those, as well as any vacations they take.

The Inside Scoop

Living at the White House might feel like living in a museum—because it is one! When she was First Lady, Jacqueline Kennedy had the White House declared a museum in order to **preserve** historic items and **furnishings**.

The First Family may redecorate parts of the White House using money set aside by Congress. Changes to historic rooms need to be approved by a committee. During President George W. Bush's second term, he and the First Lady were allowed $100,000 for changes!

They've Got It Covered

There are about 95 people in charge of the First Family's home at the White House. There are maids, a 24-hour cooking staff, and many more people who are always ready to take care of whatever the First Family needs.

When you live at the White House, you don't even have to leave to go to the doctor. There's a doctor whose job it is to take care of the president, the First Family, the vice president, and White House staff and visitors.

The Inside Scoop

Nancy Reagan said that when she lived in the White House with President Ronald Reagan, the staff was quiet and swift! "Five minutes after Ronnie came home and hung up his suit, it would disappear from the closet to be pressed, cleaned, or brushed."

Michelle Obama said that when she became First Lady, she told the staff her daughters would be making their own beds and cleaning their bedrooms. "I want the kids to be treated like children, not little princesses," she said.

Securing the White House

Members of the Secret Service add to the staff of the White House. They patrol the White House grounds and go everywhere with members of the First Family.

The White House is a safe place to live because of other security measures, too. **Commercial** planes and helicopters can't fly above the White House. The windows are bulletproof. An iron fence surrounds the White House. Many of these precautions were added after events that seemed to call the safety of the White House into question.

The Inside Scoop

The White House wasn't built to be a **fortress**. It was meant to be available to regular Americans. In fact, until World War II, the public was free to walk the White House grounds during the day.

In 1983, a bombing overseas drove the Secret Service to add concrete barriers to keep cars and people away from the White House.

Staying Inside...

Security at the White House is necessary. However, it can make the president and First Family feel **confined** and **isolated**. President Harry Truman called the White House a "**glamorous** prison."

There's also very little privacy for those who live in the White House. The First Family is constantly in the national spotlight, so leaving can be tough. First Lady Hillary Clinton would sometimes wear sunglasses, a hat, or scarves just to take a walk or go shopping so she wouldn't be recognized.

The Inside Scoop

How would you like **tourists** in your house? About 1.5 million people tour the White House each year. Countless others walk by and take pictures!

Being a public figure is hard enough. Imagine living in the most famous house in America!

You, at the White House!

Did you know regular Americans can stay overnight at the White House? These guests can see what it's like to live there!

Guests can stay one night in the Lincoln Bedroom or the Queen's Bedroom, where queens from Norway and England have stayed. Guests can use the bowling alley, movie theater, and library—but only if the president isn't using them! This reminds Americans the White House is the people's house, too.

The Inside Scoop

Abraham Lincoln's ghost has been spotted in the Lincoln Bedroom and around the White House many times over the years. Would you be scared to stay there?

White House Trivia

- Running water was first piped into the White House in 1833.

- There are 412 doors and 147 windows in the White House.

- To paint the outside of the White House, 570 gallons (2,157 l) of paint are needed.

- The White House is the oldest **federal** building in Washington, DC.

- Many of the seeds grown in the White House kitchen garden came from the Thomas Jefferson Center for Historic Plants at Monticello, Jefferson's home in Virginia.

- The Blue Room was originally decorated in red. The furnishings were first blue in 1837, and the walls were painted blue in 1902.

Glossary

commercial: having to do with business and profits

confine: to keep indoors or within other limits

federal: having to do with the national government

fortress: a place somewhat like a castle with many defenses

furnishing: decoration in a house

glamorous: full of exciting appeal

isolate: to keep apart from others

preserve: to keep safe

residence: living quarters

tourist: a person traveling to visit a place

For More Information

BOOKS

Belanger, Jeff. *Who's Haunting the White House? The President's Mansion and the Ghosts Who Live There.* New York, NY: Sterling Publishing, 2008.

House, Katherine L. *The White House for Kids: A History of a Home, Office, and National Symbol with 21 Activities.* Chicago, IL: Chicago Review Press, 2014.

WEBSITES

White House for Kids
clinton4.nara.gov/WH/kids/html/home.html
Use this website for kids to learn more about the White House. It was created while President Bill Clinton was in office.

White House Interactive Tour
www.whitehouse.gov/about/inside-white-house/interactive-tour
Explore the White House by clicking on the rooms and grounds of America's most famous home.

Publisher's note to educators and parents: Our editors have carefully reviewed these websites to ensure that they are suitable for students. Many websites change frequently, however, and we cannot guarantee that a site's future contents will continue to meet our high standards of quality and educational value. Be advised that students should be closely supervised whenever they access the Internet.

Index